Modern Idols: Unmasking Comfort

Kurt Barnes

Copyright © 2024 Kurt Barnes

All rights reserved.

ISBN: 9798344277745

DEDICATION

To my amazing family, Summer, Keegan, and Kyler.

Watch the Sermon @ scf.tv/Comfort

CONTENTS

Chapter 1: Understanding Modern Idolatry — 6

Chapter 2: The Comfort Idol in Contemporary Society — 10

Chapter 3: The Biblical Perspective on Comfort — 15

Chapter 4: Gift vs. Idol: The Fine Line — 19

Chapter 5: Recognizing the Idol of Comfort — 23

Chapter 6: Biblical Case Studies of Misplaced Comfort — 29

Chapter 7: Personal Application and Reflection — 34

Chapter 8: Practical Steps for Reordering Your Life — 43

Chapter 9: Discovering True Contentment — 49

Chapter 10: A Journey Toward Eternal Promise — 54

Additional Resources — 58

Chapter 1: Understanding Modern Idolatry

In today's fast-paced and ever-evolving world, the concept of idolatry might seem antiquated or irrelevant. However, the essence of idolatry remains strikingly pertinent. It begins with understanding what truly constitutes an idol in our modern lives. Drawing on wisdom from theologians like Tim Keller, who defines an idol as "anything more important to you than God, anything that absorbs your heart and your imagination more than God, anything you seek to give you what only God can give," we embark on a journey to uncover these subtle, yet significant, influences.

The Nature of Idols

At its core, an idol is anything or anyone that takes precedence over our relationship with God. This definition extends beyond the primitive idea of statues or carved figures. In contemporary society, idols are often intangible, embedded deeply in our desires, priorities, and the objects of our devotion. They are the things that command our attention, govern our actions, and shape our identity, often without us even realizing their power over us.

Idols in Modern Life

Today's idols are sleek and sophisticated, often disguised as virtues or necessities. They frequently manifest in various forms, such as:

- **Material Success**: The relentless pursuit of wealth and status, believing that financial security will bring ultimate fulfillment.

- **Personal Comfort**: Prioritizing ease and pleasure, leading to a reluctance to engage in activities that require sacrifice or discomfort.

- **Relationships**: Elevating romantic partners, family, or friends to a pedestal where their opinions and presence dictate one's self-worth and decisions.

- **Technology and Entertainment**: Allowing digital devices or the consumption of media to dominate our time and influence our perspectives, often numbing us to deeper spiritual engagements.
- **Self-Image**: Fixation on personal appearance, achievements, or reputation can lead to an identity crisis rooted in how others perceive us rather than how God sees us.

The Deceptive Allure of Idolatry

Idols promise satisfaction and fulfillment, yet they invariably fail to deliver these in any lasting form. They create a cycle of dependency, where the initial joy or contentment they provide is fleeting, pushing us to seek more and more, often at the expense of our spiritual health and relationships. This deceptive allure turns gifts, meant to be enjoyed with gratitude, into gods that demand our worship and obedience.

Recognizing and Addressing Idols

Identifying idols requires introspection and honesty. It involves asking ourselves critical questions: What consumes my thoughts regularly? Where do I turn for comfort and security? What am I willing to make sacrifices for, even to the point of compromising my values or beliefs?

Once recognized, addressing these idols involves a reorientation of our hearts and minds towards God. It necessitates repentance, a conscious decision to place God at the center of our lives, and a commitment to engage with His truth daily. By doing so, we reclaim the space in our hearts that belongs solely to the Creator, enabling us to enjoy His gifts without them becoming detrimental to our spiritual journey.

Conclusion

In this modern era, where distractions and diversions abound, understanding and identifying idols is the first step toward spiritual clarity and freedom. As we continue this exploration, it becomes evident that only by acknowledging and dismantling these idols can we truly live a life aligned with God's purpose and filled with His everlasting peace.

Questions:

1. What are the most important things in your life, and how do they compare to your relationship with God?

   _____
   _____
   _____
   _____
   _____
   _____

2. Have you ever recognized a modern idol in your life? How did it affect your relationship with God?

   _____
   _____
   _____
   _____
   _____
   _____

3. In what ways can things that don't seem inherently bad become idols?

   _____
   _____
   _____
   _____
   _____
   _____

Activities:

- **Self-Inventory:** List the top five priorities in your life and evaluate each one's impact on your spiritual health.

   _____
   _____
   _____
   _____

- **Reflection Exercise:** Spend ten minutes in quiet reflection or prayer, asking God to reveal any idols that may be occupying your heart.

Chapter 2: The Comfort Idol in Contemporary Society

As we delve deeper into the landscape of modern idolatry, we find that comfort emerges as a particularly dominant force. It is woven into the fabric of our daily lives, informing decisions, shaping lifestyles, and often defining success. The desire for comfort, both physical and emotional, is so pervasive that it topped the list in a Lifeway Christian Research survey on modern idols affecting congregations. But how did comfort attain such an exalted status, and what are its cultural ramifications?

The Rise of the Comfort Idol

Historically, comfort was a luxury, often reserved for moments of respite from labor or struggle. Today, however, comfort has transitioned from luxury to expectation. This shift is driven by technology, economic advancements, and socio-cultural changes that prioritize convenience and ease. Modern amenities and innovations—from smart home devices to on-demand services—have revolutionized our environment, making daily life more comfortable than ever before.

Cultural Phenomena and the Idolization of Comfort

One of the most striking cultural embodiments of this phenomenon is the Danish concept of "hygge" (pronounced "hue-gah"). This lifestyle trend, which emphasizes coziness, warmth, and contentment, has captured global attention. While hygge encourages simple pleasures and mindfulness, its widespread popularity reflects a deeper, almost aspirational longing for uninterrupted comfort. It presents an ideal where discomfort is not just minimized but avoided altogether.

The global embrace of hygge has further cemented the idea that comfort is not merely desirable but necessary. It has implications on consumer habits, fueling industries that promise solace and convenience, such as fashion, interior design, and leisure activities.

The Implications of Pursuing Comfort

While the pursuit of comfort is not inherently negative, its elevation to an idol poses significant challenges. When comfort becomes central, discomfort is perceived as a threat to be eliminated. This mindset can lead to several societal and personal implications:

- **Avoidance of Growth**: Genuine growth often requires stepping out of comfort zones. When comfort is idolized, there is a tendency to shy away from challenges that foster personal and spiritual development.

- **Emphasis on Immediate Gratification**: The cultural shift towards comfort fosters a preference for quick fixes and instant results, undermining the value of perseverance and long-term commitment.

- **Erosion of Resilience**: An overemphasis on comfort can diminish resilience, making individuals less equipped to handle adversity or cope with the unpredictability's of life.

- **Spiritual Apathy**: In the spiritual realm, prioritizing comfort can lead to a stagnant faith, where one's relationship with God is driven more by personal convenience than by conviction or devotion.

Evaluating the Effects of Comfort

The data from Lifeway Christian Research underscores the significant impact of comfort as an idol within congregations. Pastors report that this preoccupation with comfort affects worship attendance, volunteerism, and engagement with spiritual disciplines—all areas where sacrifice and commitment are often required.

Addressing this idol involves reintroducing the value of discomfort—in moderation—as a pathway to growth and deeper fulfillment. It encourages embracing challenges when they align with God's purposes and values, understanding that true contentment and peace are found in faith, rather than the trappings of comfort.

Conclusion

As we navigate a world that increasingly idolizes comfort, it is essential to critically assess its place in our lives. Recognizing its influence allows us to reclaim the joy in spiritual resilience and growth. By realigning our priorities, we can appreciate comfort for what it truly is—a gift from God, meant to soothe and restore, but never to replace the fulfillment that comes from a life devoted wholly to Him.

Questions:

1. How does your pursuit of comfort affect your relationships, priorities, and lifestyle?

   _____
   _____
   _____
   _____
   _____
   _____

2. What aspects of your life reflect cultural trends like "hygge"? Do they align with your values?

   _____
   _____
   _____
   _____
   _____
   _____

3. How can the pursuit of comfort detract from spiritual growth and resilience?

   _____
   _____
   _____
   _____
   _____
   _____

Activities:

- **Cultural Analysis:** Write a short essay analyzing how societal trends influence your views on comfort.

- **Comfort Fast:** Choose a comfort item or habit to temporarily give up, using the experience to assess its hold on your life.

Chapter 3: The Biblical Perspective on Comfort

To fully understand the concept of comfort and its place in our lives, we must turn to Scripture, which offers profound insights into God's original design for comfort and His ultimate promise of its restoration. The Bible paints a picture of comfort as both a divine provision and a foretaste of the eternal harmony intended for humanity.

God's Original Design for Comfort

In the beginning, the Garden of Eden epitomized God's perfect provision of comfort. Genesis describes a paradise where physical and emotional needs were abundantly met. In Genesis 2:8-9, we read, "Now the Lord God had planted a garden in the east, in Eden; and there he put the man he had formed. The Lord God made all kinds of trees grow out of the ground—trees that were pleasing to the eye and good for food." This passage illustrates a world where physical nourishment was plentiful and aesthetically pleasing, reflecting God's desire for humanity to enjoy both sustenance and beauty.

Moreover, emotional comfort was inherent in the relationships God designed. God's recognition of Adam's need for companionship in Genesis 2:18—"It is not good for the man to be alone. I will make a helper suitable for him"—highlights God's attention to emotional well-being. The creation of Eve signified the importance of relational intimacy and support, fundamental aspects of emotional comfort.

The Promise of Comfort's Restoration

While humanity's fall introduced pain, suffering, and the distortion of God's original design, Scripture gives us hope by promising the eventual restoration of comfort. Revelation 21:3-4 offers a vision of this renewal: "And I heard a loud voice from the throne saying, 'Look! God's dwelling place is now among the people, and he will dwell with them. They will be his people, and God himself will be with them and be their God. He will wipe every tear from their eyes. There will be no more death or mourning or crying or pain, for the old order of things has passed away.'"

This prophecy reassures us of a future devoid of pain and suffering, where both physical and emotional comforts are perfectly restored. God's presence among His people will eliminate sorrow and discomfort, fulfilling the original plan for humanity to live in unbroken harmony with Him.

Biblical Provisions for Comfort Today

Even in a fallen world, God continues to provide comfort for His children, both physically and emotionally. Matthew 6:31-33 reminds us of God's attentive provision: "So do not worry, saying, 'What shall we eat?' or 'What shall we drink?' or 'What shall we wear?' For the pagans run after all these things, and your heavenly Father knows that you need them. But seek first his kingdom and his righteousness, and all these things will be given to you as well." Here, Jesus assures us of God's provision for our physical needs, encouraging a life of trust and prioritizing spiritual pursuits.

For emotional comfort, 2 Corinthians 1:3-4 declares, "Praise be to the God and Father of our Lord Jesus Christ, the Father of compassion and the God of all comfort, who comforts us in all our troubles, so that we can comfort those in any trouble with the comfort we ourselves receive from God." This passage emphasizes God's role as the ultimate source of comfort, enabling us to extend His compassion to others, creating a community of support and encouragement.

Responding to God's Gift of Comfort

Understanding comfort through a biblical lens challenges us to reposition it within God's framework, acknowledging Him as its true source. It calls us to appreciate the comforts we experience now as gifts, leading us to worship and thanksgiving rather than idolatry.

Conclusion

The biblical narrative shows that God's blueprint for comfort is integrally woven into His relationship with humanity. As we strive toward the restoration promised in Revelation, we find assurance in God's ongoing presence and provision. By embracing His original design and future promise, we align ourselves with His purpose, allowing comfort to enhance our relationship with Him rather than overshadow it.

Questions:

1. What does the Garden of Eden teach us about God's original intent for comfort?

   _____
   _____
   _____
   _____
   _____
   _____

2. How does the promise of future restoration in Revelation influence your current understanding of comfort?

   _____
   _____
   _____
   _____
   _____

3. Reflect on a time God provided comfort during a challenging period. How did it impact your faith?

   _____
   _____
   _____
   _____
   _____
   _____

Activities:

- **Scripture Study:** Compare the descriptions of comfort in Genesis and Revelation, noting how they inform each other.

- **Prayer Journal:** Record times in your life when you've experienced God's comfort and reflect on these instances in prayer.

Chapter 4: Gift vs. Idol: The Fine Line

Life is filled with blessings that are meant to enhance our journey, bringing joy, fulfillment, and opportunities to worship God for His generosity. However, the challenge lies in distinguishing between enjoying these gifts as they were intended and elevating them to a status where they become idols that compete with God for our loyalty and affection. This chapter delves into the subtle yet profound difference between a gift and an idol, offering insights into how to maintain the intended balance.

Understanding God's Gifts

God's gifts, encompassing elements such as food, rest, relationships, and material blessings, are meant to be experiences that draw us closer to Him through gratitude and contentment. James 1:17 emphasizes this, stating, "Every good and perfect gift is from above, coming down from the Father of the heavenly lights, who does not change like shifting shadows." Here, gifts are seen as reflections of God's unwavering goodness and kindness.

Food, for instance, is more than sustenance; it's an opportunity to appreciate God's creativity and provision. Relationships offer companionship and support, mirroring the love and community found within the Trinity. Rest provides restoration, allowing us to recharge and engage more fully with life and God's calling.

The Path to Idolatry

Despite their goodness, these gifts can be distorted into idols. The transition from gift to idol often occurs subtly, when a good thing assumes an ultimate place in our hearts. This distortion is captured in Romans 1:25, which states, "They exchanged the truth about God for a lie, and worshiped and served created things rather than the Creator—who is forever praised. Amen."

The idolatry of food, for example, might manifest in gluttony or an unhealthy obsession with dieting and appearance. Relationships can become idols when we place our worth and identity entirely in others' hands, often leading to codependency or manipulation. Rest can transform into laziness or avoidance of responsibility.

Indicators of Idolatry

A gift becomes an idol when it begins to dictate our actions and emotions, leading us away from God's commands and purposes. Some indicators that can help distinguish this include:

- **Prioritization Over God**: When a gift takes precedence over spiritual disciplines, such as prayer and worship, it has likely become an idol.

- **Willingness to Sin**: As posed by the litmus test in Tim Keller's definition, if we are willing to sin to obtain or keep something, it indicates that the gift has assumed idol status.

- **Emotional Dependency**: If our emotional stability is disproportionately affected by the presence or absence of a gift, it reveals an unhealthy attachment.

Returning to Worship

To realign our hearts, we must return to a posture of worship and gratitude, acknowledging God as the source of all good things. This involves:

- **Cultivating Gratitude**: Regularly thanking God for His gifts fosters a mindset of appreciation rather than entitlement or obsession.

- **Setting Boundaries**: Establishing limits on how we engage with God's gifts helps prevent them from becoming consuming forces in our lives.

- **Re-prioritization**: Actively prioritizing God's commands and desires over personal gratification ensures that our loyalty remains with Him.

Conclusion

God's gracious gifts are designed to enrich our lives and serve as reminders of His love and provision. By recognizing and resisting the temptation to idolize these blessings, we maintain the intended balance that allows us to enjoy God's world without compromising our relationship with Him. Through vigilance and heart realignment, we uphold a life of worship and devotion, celebrating the Giver above the gifts.

Questions:

1. How can you enjoy the gifts God has given without turning them into idols?

2. Are there gifts in your life that have become more important than your relationship with God?

3. How can you distinguish between healthy enjoyment and idolatry?

Activities:

- **Gift Audit:** List the gifts in your life and assess whether any have taken on undue importance.

- **Thanksgiving Reflection:** Write a prayer of thanksgiving for God's gifts, focusing on the purpose each one serves in your life.

Chapter 5: Recognizing the Idol of Comfort

In our quest to identify modern idols, comfort stands out as one that is both alluring and potentially consuming. Unlike overtly negative influences, comfort often masquerades as a harmless or even necessary pursuit. Yet, when misaligned, it can quietly assume a dominant role in our lives. This chapter aims to equip you with practical insights and self-reflection tools to discern when comfort has crossed the line from a healthy enjoyment to an idol.

The Subtlety of Comfort as an Idol

Comfort, by nature, is not easily recognized as an idol. It is an appealing state that offers relief from stress and hardship, often justified as a reward or necessity. However, when the pursuit or protection of comfort begins to interfere with our spiritual responsibilities and growth, it requires evaluation.

Litmus Test 1: "Will I Sin to Get It?"

One of the most telling indicators of idolatry is whether we are willing to compromise our values, integrity, or obedience to God in pursuit of comfort. Consider asking yourself:

- **Am I circumventing God's commands to maintain my comfort?** For instance, if avoiding discomfort leads you to deceit, neglect of responsibilities, or omission of truths, it suggests that comfort holds excessive sway in your life.
- **Do I prioritize my ease over God's call to self-sacrifice?** Comfort can become an idol when it keeps us from engaging in acts of service, generosity, or missions that involve risk or sacrifice.

Litmus Test 2: "Will I Sin if I Don't Get It?"

Our reactions to denied comfort can also reveal idolatry. Reflect on these points:

- **How do I respond to discomfort or inconvenience?** Excessive anger, frustration, or despair might indicate that comfort has taken on more importance than it should.

- **Do I resist God's plans when they involve discomfort or uncertainty?** When we choose personal comfort over God's direction, it can hinder our spiritual growth and obedience.

Self-Reflection Tools for Discerning Idolatry

To further aid in recognizing comfort as an idol, engage with these self-reflective practices:

1. **Journaling**: Regularly document situations where comfort significantly influences your decisions. Look for patterns where comfort takes priority over God-directed actions.

2. **Prayer and Meditation**: Invite God to reveal areas where comfort has become an idol. Praying for discernment and openness can provide the clarity needed to address misplaced priorities.

3. **Accountability**: Share your intentions and struggles with a trusted friend or mentor. They can offer insights and hold you accountable to ensure comfort remains a balanced part of your life.

4. **Revisit Scripture**: Study biblical passages that speak to the balance of comfort and sacrifice, such as Matthew 16:24-26, where Jesus calls His followers to take up their cross.

Reorienting Comfort Within God's Framework

Once identified, reorienting comfort involves intentionally placing it within the context of God's purposes:

- **Embrace Discomfort as Growth**: Recognize that discomfort often accompanies growth and deeper reliance on God. Embracing it can lead to spiritual maturity and resilience.

- **Align Comfort with Kingdom Goals**: Ensure that your pursuit of comfort aligns with, rather than opposes, God's will. Let comfort be a means to enhance your ability to serve others and glorify God.

Conclusion

By applying these litmus tests and self-reflection tools, you can maintain a healthy relationship with comfort, ensuring it remains a gift rather than an obstacle. As we continue to seek God's kingdom first, we learn that true comfort is ultimately found not in temporary ease, but in the eternal peace and presence of God.

Questions:

1. Can you identify recent decisions where comfort influenced your actions? How did it affect your obedience to God's directives?

_____
_____
_____
_____
_____
_____
_____
_____
_____
_____
_____
_____

2. How do you typically react when faced with situations that challenge your comfort? Are there patterns of behavior that suggest idolatry?

_____
_____
_____
_____
_____

Modern Idols

3. In what areas of your life might comfort be hindering your willingness to sacrifice for God's call or for others?

___

4. Do you experience fear or anxiety at the thought of losing certain comforts? What does this reveal about their importance in your life?

___

Activities:

1. Spend a week documenting instances where the desire for comfort influenced your choices. Reflect on these entries to identify patterns and consider alternative responses that align with God's guidance.

___

Modern Idols

2. Dedicate time to praying for insight and courage to recognize areas where comfort acts as an idol. Meditate on Bible verses that emphasize reliance on God, such as Philippians 4:6-7.

3. Identify one comfort you frequently seek and commit to temporarily abstaining from it. Use this period to intentionally seek God's guidance and see how reliance on Him during discomfort can strengthen your faith.

Modern Idols

Chapter 6: Biblical Case Studies of Misplaced Comfort

Throughout Scripture, we find vivid examples of how the gifts intended to be blessings can become idols, leading individuals away from God's commands. These stories serve as timeless lessons, illustrating the potential pitfalls of idolizing comfort and the consequences that follow.

David and Bathsheba: The Comfort of Power

King David's encounter with Bathsheba is a stark reminder of how the idol of comfort, fueled by power and privilege, can lead to devastating moral failures. The narrative begins in 2 Samuel 11:1-4:

"In the spring, at the time when kings go off to war, David sent Joab out with the king's men and the whole Israelite army. They destroyed the Ammonites and besieged Rabbah. But David remained in Jerusalem. One evening David got up from his bed and walked around on the roof of the palace. From the roof, he saw a woman bathing. The woman was very beautiful, and David sent someone to find out about her."

David, who had experienced God's blessing of kingship, became complacent, indulging in the comfort and power that his position offered. Instead of leading his troops as was customary, he stayed behind, succumbing to idleness. This choice of comfort over duty set the stage for adultery, deceit, and eventually murder.

By prioritizing personal desires over obedience, David exemplified how the comfort of power can distort judgment and lead to grave consequences, ultimately causing turmoil in his family and kingdom. Yet, his story also highlights the path to redemption through confession and repentance, as seen in Psalm 51.

The Israelites in the Wilderness: The Idol of Predictability

Another poignant example is the Israelites' journey through the wilderness, where the idol of comfort manifested as a longing for predictability and ease. In Exodus 16:2-3, we see their grumbling:

"In the desert the whole community grumbled against Moses and Aaron. The Israelites said to them, 'If only we had died by the Lord's hand in Egypt! There we sat around pots of meat and ate all the food we wanted, but you have brought us out into this desert to starve this entire assembly to death.'"

Despite experiencing miraculous deliverance from slavery and God's provision of manna and quail, the Israelites idolized their former life's predictability, longing for the comfort of regular meals over the uncertainties of their freedom journey. This idolatry led to widespread disobedience and a generation's delay in entering the Promised Land.

This narrative illustrates the danger of allowing past comforts to overshadow God's future promises, emphasizing the importance of trust and obedience even amidst uncertainty.

The Danger of Misplaced Hope

Both David and the Israelites demonstrate the consequences of fixating on worldly comforts, whether power, predictability, or sustenance. Their experiences reveal how such fixations can lead to moral and spiritual failures, distancing them from God's intentions.

These stories caution against allowing God's gifts to become more vital than God Himself. They remind us of the necessity of aligning comforts with God's commands, ensuring they serve as tools for glorifying Him rather than becoming ends in themselves.

Lessons for Today

From these biblical accounts, we learn that recognizing the potential for gifts to become idols is an ongoing process. It requires vigilance, humility, and a commitment to place God's will above our personal comforts. We must remember that true fulfillment lies not in the gifts themselves but in the Giver, who provides all we need for our journey.

Conclusion

Scripture's rich tapestry of stories provides more than warnings; it offers hope and guidance for realigning our hearts. By embracing discomfort when aligning with God's purposes and remaining vigilant against the subtle rise of idols, we engage in a lifelong journey of growth, transformation, and deeper dependence on God. These narratives of the past can shape our present responses and future directions, helping us live lives fully devoted to God's glory.

Questions:

1. How do the stories of David and Bathsheba and the Israelites in the wilderness resonate with your own experiences?

   _____
   _____
   _____
   _____
   _____
   _____

2. What lessons can you take from these biblical narratives to apply in your life today?

   _____
   _____
   _____
   _____
   _____
   _____

3. How do these stories shape your understanding of the consequences of turning gifts into idols?

   _____
   _____
   _____
   _____
   _____
   _____

Activities:

- **Character Study:** Write a character analysis of David or the Israelites, focusing on their relationship with comfort and its consequences.

Modern Idols

- **Group Discussion:** With a group or partner, discuss what modern-day situations could be analogous to these biblical narratives.

Chapter 7: Personal Application and Reflection

Having explored the concept of comfort as an idol and examined biblical examples of its impact, it's time to turn inward. This chapter invites you to engage in personal reflection, encouraging an honest assessment of your life to identify potential idols. Through guided questions and exercises, you can begin to realign your priorities with God's will, cultivating a heart fully devoted to Him.

Reflecting on Personal Comfort

Begin by reflecting on where comfort plays a role in your life. Consider the following questions:

1. **What areas of my life do I prioritize comfort over God's calling?**

Reflect on instances where your choices may compromise your spiritual convictions for the sake of preserving comfort.

_____
_____
_____
_____
_____
_____
_____
_____
_____
_____
_____
_____
_____
_____
_____
_____
_____

Modern Idols

2. **How do I react when comfort is disrupted?**

Evaluate your emotional responses to uncomfortable situations. Are there signs of impatience, frustration, or anger that might point to misplaced priorities?

_____
_____
_____
_____
_____
_____
_____
_____
_____
_____

3. **Have I ever compromised my values to maintain comfort?**

Think about situations where preserving comfort led you to actions or decisions that contradict your beliefs or standards.

_____
_____
_____
_____
_____
_____
_____
_____
_____
_____
_____

Identifying Potential Idols

To further examine if comfort has become an idol, engage in the following exercises:

- **Create a Comfort Inventory**: List the aspects of your life where comfort is most prevalent. This could include material possessions, relationships, or habits. Then evaluate whether any of these might overshadow your commitment to God.

_____
_____
_____
_____
_____
_____
_____
_____
_____
_____
_____
_____
_____
_____
_____
_____

- **Conduct a Time Audit**: For one week, track how you spend your time, noting activities centered around comfort versus those focused on spiritual growth. Analyze the balance and look for areas that might need adjustment.

_____
_____
_____
_____
_____
_____
_____
_____

- **Heart Check Prayer**: Spend time in prayer, asking God to reveal any hidden idols. Be open to His gentle conviction and ready to make the necessary changes to align more closely with His will.

Realigning with God's Will

The journey of realignment is ongoing and requires intentional steps to ensure God remains at the center of your life. Consider these practical strategies:

- **Set Spiritual Goals**: Develop clear goals that prioritize spiritual growth, such as daily Scripture reading, volunteering, or participating in church activities. These goals can help reorient your focus from comfort to conscientious engagement with your faith.

- **Practice Gratitude**: Regularly thank God for His gifts, maintaining a perspective that sees comfort as a blessing, not a necessity. Gratitude fosters contentment and keeps your heart attuned to God's provision.

- **Embrace Discomfort**: Challenge yourself to step out of comfort zones occasionally. Volunteering for tasks that stretch your abilities or engaging with communities outside your usual circle can provide new opportunities for growth and reliance on God.

- **Seek Community Accountability**: Join a small group or find an accountability partner who can offer support and encouragement in maintaining your commitments to God over comfort.

Reflective Journaling Exercise

Dedicate time each week to journal about your progress. Contemplate these prompts:

- **How has my understanding of comfort changed?**

_____
_____
_____
_____
_____
_____
_____
_____
_____
_____
_____
_____
_____
_____

- **What steps have I taken to prioritize God's will over my comfort?**

- **In what ways have I experienced God's presence and guidance in this journey?**

Conclusion

Identifying and overcoming the idol of comfort is a deeply personal and transformative process. By continuously reflecting, seeking God's guidance, and implementing intentional changes, you can cultivate a life that prioritizes His will over worldly comforts. This journey not only deepens your relationship with God but also introduces a richer understanding of true contentment and fulfillment. As you continue to align your life with God's purposes, embrace the promise of His abundant grace and unwavering presence on this journey.

Questions:

1. Which aspects of your life might have become idols?

2. How do your priorities align with God's will?

___

3. What changes can you make to better align your life with God's purposes?

___

Activities:

- **Priority Evaluation:** Create a list of current priorities and rate them by their alignment with spiritual values.

___

- **Guided Reflection:** Set aside a time for prayerful reflection on your priorities, seeking God's guidance in reordering them.

Chapter 8: Practical Steps for Reordering Your Life

Transitioning from a life centered around the idol of comfort to a God-centered existence involves intentional actions and a willingness to embrace change. This chapter offers practical steps that encourage a shift in focus, guiding you toward a life marked by gratitude and obedience to God.

Step 1: Cultivate a Heart of Gratitude

Gratitude is foundational for reordering your life around God. By recognizing and appreciating His gifts, you align your heart with His presence and provisions.

- **Daily Gratitude Practice**: Begin each day by listing three things you are thankful for, focusing on both the blessings and the challenges that bring growth. This practice fosters a mindset of appreciation, redirecting your focus from what you lack to what you have received.

- **Thanksgiving Journal**: Keep a journal dedicated to recording moments of gratitude. Reflect on how God has provided, guided, and comforted you, continuously reminding yourself of His faithfulness.

Step 2: Prioritize Spiritual Disciplines

Engaging consistently in spiritual disciplines strengthens your relationship with God and reduces the allure of comfort as an idol.

- **Set a Regular Prayer Schedule**: Allocate specific times each day for prayer, cultivating a deeper conversational relationship with God. Prayer offers solace beyond physical comfort, providing spiritual peace and clarity.

- **Immerse in Scripture**: Engage deeply with the Bible through study or devotional plans. The insights and wisdom gained from

Scripture can reorient your priorities and strengthen your commitment to God's will.

Step 3: Embrace Obedience through Action

Obedience is a testament to prioritizing God over personal comfort. Actively seek opportunities to align your actions with His commands.

- **Serve Others**: Volunteer for activities or organizations that align with God's compassion and justice. Serving others shifts your focus from self-centered comfort to outward-looking love.

- **Practice Self-Discipline**: Identify areas where comfort has hindered your spiritual growth, and set boundaries to counteract it. This could involve limiting screen time or fasting from certain comforts to refocus your heart on God.

Step 4: Engage in Community

Community offers accountability and support, vital components for sustaining a God-centered life.

- **Join a Small Group**: Participate in a small group where you can share your journey, receive encouragement, and hold each other accountable. This communal engagement enriches your spiritual outlook and provides shared wisdom.

- **Mentorship**: Seek a mentor or become one. A mentor can offer guidance and perspective, while mentoring others provides an avenue to share God's love and teach what you've learned.

Step 5: Reflect and Reassess Regularly

Periodically evaluate your spiritual journey to ensure continued alignment with God's purposes.

- **Weekly Reflection**: Set aside time each week to reflect on your progress. Ask yourself: How have I prioritized God this week? What challenges have I faced, and how did I respond?

- **Monthly Spiritual Retreats**: Dedicate a day each month for quiet reflection and communion with God. Use this time to seek His direction for the coming month and commit to any necessary changes or new goals.

Conclusion

Shifting focus from the idol of comfort to a God-centered life is an ongoing journey requiring intention and dedication. By incorporating gratitude, engaging in spiritual disciplines, embracing obedience, fostering community, and regularly reassessing your journey, you can cultivate a lifestyle that resonates with God's love and purpose. Through these practical steps, you not only grow closer to God but also experience a deeper, more fulfilling sense of peace and joy that transcends temporary comforts.

Questions:

1. Which practical steps resonate most with you, and why?

2. What barriers do you foresee when implementing these steps?

3. How can you effectively maintain a focus on God's will over personal comfort?

Activities:

- **Action Plan:** Develop a personalized plan to implement at least two steps, setting specific goals and measures of accountability.

_____
_____
_____
_____
_____
_____
_____
_____
_____
_____
_____
_____
_____
_____
_____
_____
_____

- **Community Engagement:** Join a spiritual group or class that supports your growth in prioritizing God.

_____
_____
_____
_____
_____
_____
_____
_____
_____
_____
_____
_____
_____

Modern Idols

Chapter 9: Discovering True Contentment

In a world where contentment is often equated with material wealth, status, or comfort, finding genuine satisfaction that transcends these external factors is a profound pursuit. This chapter explores the essence of true contentment, grounded in God's presence and nurtured through spiritual disciplines and community support, offering deeper joy that surpasses worldly comforts.

The Nature of True Contentment

True contentment is not a state of having everything but a state of recognizing that you are enough and have enough because of your relationship with God. Philippians 4:11-13 provides insight into this profound truth through the Apostle Paul, who writes, "I have learned to be content whatever the circumstances. I know what it is to be in need, and I know what it is to have plenty. I have learned the secret of being content in any and every situation... I can do all this through him who gives me strength." Here, contentment is described as an inner peace and sufficiency found in Christ, irrespective of external situations.

Cultivating Spiritual Disciplines

Spiritual disciplines are instrumental in fostering this deeper contentment. They provide a structure through which we can experience God's presence more intimately and consistently.

- **Prayer and Meditation**: Regularly spending time in prayer and meditation on God's word centers your heart on His peace. Practicing mindfulness of His presence throughout your day enhances awareness and appreciation for His ongoing work in your life.

- **Scripture Study**: Deep engagement with the Bible unveils the richness of God's promises and truths, reinforcing your identity and purpose in Him. Scripture offers guidance and wisdom that cultivates contentment beyond the temporary satisfaction of worldly goods.

- **Worship and Praise**: Worship focuses your attention on God's goodness and power, fostering gratitude and joy independent of your circumstances. Engaging in both personal and communal worship cultivates a heart that finds joy in celebrating who God is.

The Role of Community Support

Community provides essential support and encouragement in sustaining contentment, reminding us of the relational aspect of God's design.

- **Fellowship**: Sharing life with fellow believers offers encouragement and perspective, especially during challenging times. The testimonies and experiences of others can reinforce your trust in God's provision and plan.

- **Accountability**: Having someone to hold you accountable helps maintain focus on spiritual goals and discourages the tendencies to seek contentment in fleeting comforts. This mutual encouragement strengthens resilience against the idolatry of external comforts.

- **Service and Contribution**: Actively participating in serving others turns the focus outward, fostering a sense of purpose and contentment in fulfilling God's calling to love and support one another.

Practicing Gratitude and Simplicity

Embodying gratitude for what you have and pursuing simplicity dethrones the false promises of material contentment.

- **Gratitude Rituals**: Daily or weekly rituals of expressing thanks to God, whether through journaling, prayer, or conversation, shift your focus from wants to blessings, nurturing contentment in all circumstances.

- **Embracing Simplicity**: Practicing simplicity in lifestyle choices reduces dependency on material possessions for happiness.

Evaluate what truly brings joy and let go of excess that distracts from a God-centered life.

Conclusion

Ultimately, true contentment is a transformative journey rooted in the assurance found in God's presence. By cultivating spiritual disciplines and engaging in community support, you unlock a deeper joy that is steadfast, irrespective of life's external fluctuations. This contentment enriches your life with lasting fulfillment, aligning your heart with God's eternal perspective and purpose. As you pursue this path, you discover that God's presence is the greatest treasure, satisfying your soul beyond the confines of the world's fleeting comforts.

Questions:

1. What does true contentment look like in your life?

_____
_____
_____
_____
_____
_____
_____
_____
_____
_____
_____
_____
_____
_____
_____
_____
_____
_____
_____
_____

2. How can spiritual disciplines enhance your sense of contentment?

3. What role does community play in fostering contentment?

Activities:

- **Contentment Journal:** Write regularly about moments when you felt true contentment and how they correlate with your spiritual practices.

_____
_____
_____
_____
_____
_____
_____
_____
_____
_____
_____
_____
_____
_____
_____
_____
_____

- **Community Engagement Exercise:** Organize or join a group activity aimed at serving others to experience the joy of outward-focused life.

Chapter 10: A Journey Toward Eternal Promise

As we conclude this exploration of comfort, idolatry, and spiritual alignment, it is essential to anchor our hearts in the hope and assurance that God offers. The journey of identifying and reordering comfort in our lives is not just a call away from idolatry but a call toward the deeper, enduring promises of God's grace and the ultimate restoration that awaits us.

The Assurance of God's Grace

First and foremost, remember that this journey begins and ends with God's grace. His grace meets us at every point of our walk, whether in moments of triumph or struggle. Hebrews 4:16 encourages us: "Let us then approach God's throne of grace with confidence, so that we may receive mercy and find grace to help us in our time of need." God's grace empowers us to recognize and overcome the idols in our lives, offering forgiveness and strength as we strive to live in alignment with His will.

The Promise of Restoration

The Bible assures us of an eternal future where all things are restored to their perfect state. Revelation 21:4 paints a compelling picture of this promise: "He will wipe every tear from their eyes. There will be no more death or mourning or crying or pain, for the old order of things has passed away." This vision of the new heaven and earth reminds us that our current experiences of comfort are but a shadow of the complete fulfillment and joy that are promised to us in eternity.

In heaven, we will experience God's original design for comfort, where physical and emotional well-being are fully realized in His presence. This assurance provides hope and perspective, reminding us that our ultimate contentment and comfort lie not in earthly pursuits but in the divine promise of eternal life with God.

Encouragement to Pursue God's Promises

In light of these truths, we are called to pursue a life that is centered on God's eternal promises. Here are final encouragements to guide this pursuit:

- **Live with Eternal Perspective**: Let the assurance of heavenly restoration influence your daily life. Prioritize what has lasting value over temporary pleasures, focusing on building a legacy of faith and love.
- **Embrace God's Presence Now**: Seek to live in daily awareness of God's presence and provision. Cultivate gratitude and joy in the moments where His comfort appears, knowing that each is a glimpse of the fullness to come.
- **Share the Hope**: Extend this hope and encouragement to others. Share the promises of God with those journeying alongside you, offering support and testimony of His grace in your life.
- **Endure in Faith**: Keep moving forward, even when challenged. The journey may not always be smooth, but persistence rooted in faith keeps one aligned with God's purposes and leads to growth and deeper reliance on Him.

Conclusion

As you conclude this exploration, may you carry forward the message of hope and encouragement that God's grace brings. Know that your journey is significant and that each step towards prioritizing God navigates you closer to His eternal promises. Celebrate the assurance that one day, all comfort will be restored, and every longing fulfilled in His glorious presence. Until then, let this pursuit of a God-centered life bring profound joy, freedom, and meaningful transformation, as you live confidently in the truth of His eternal love and the promise of heaven.

Questions:

1. How does the promise of restoration shape your current pursuits and priorities?

Modern Idols

2. What aspects of God's grace most influence your journey toward a God-centered life?

3. How can you actively share the hope of God's promises with others?

Activities:

- **Hope Map:** Create a visual representation of your spiritual journey, highlighting key moments of God's influence and grace.

- **Encouragement Task:** Write a letter of encouragement to someone else who is navigating their spiritual journey, incorporating insights from this exploration.

Additional Resources:

5-day Bible reading plan and devotional:

Day 1: The Source of True Comfort

Reading: Psalm 23:1-6

Devotional: As we begin this journey, let's reflect on the ultimate source of our comfort. In Psalm 23, David paints a beautiful picture of God as our shepherd, providing for our every need. Just as God designed the Garden of Eden to be a place of perfect comfort for Adam and Eve, He desires to be our comfort in this imperfect world. Today, consider the areas of your life where you're seeking comfort outside of God. Are there created things that have taken His place? Remember, every good gift comes from Him, but He alone should be our ultimate source of comfort. Take time to thank God for His provision and ask Him to help you find your deepest comfort in His presence.

Day 2: Comfort in God's Promises

Reading: Matthew 6:25-34

Devotional: Jesus reminds us in this passage that our Heavenly Father knows our needs and cares for us deeply. When we prioritize seeking God's kingdom, He promises to provide for our physical and emotional needs. However, we often fall into the trap of worrying about these things, much like the Israelites did in the wilderness. Reflect on areas where worry has taken root in your life. How might trusting in God's promises bring you comfort? Today, practice surrendering your anxieties to God and actively seeking His kingdom first. Let His promises be your source of comfort rather than the temporary securities of this world.

Day 3: The Danger of Misplaced Comfort

Reading: Romans 1:21-25

Devotional: Paul warns us about the human tendency to worship created things rather than the Creator. This passage reminds us how easily we can turn good gifts from God into idols. Consider the comforts in your life – your home, relationships, food, entertainment. While these are blessings from God, have any of them become so central to your life that losing them would feel unbearable? Today, examine your heart and ask God to reveal any areas where you might be elevating His gifts above Him. Pray for the wisdom to enjoy His blessings without making them the source of your ultimate comfort and security.

Day 4: Finding Comfort in Suffering

Reading: 2 Corinthians 1:3-7

Devotional: In this passage, Paul reminds us that God is the source of all comfort, even in our troubles. Remarkably, our sufferings can become a means through which we comfort others. Reflect on a time when God comforted you in a difficult situation. How might that experience equip you to comfort someone else? Today, if you're going through a challenging time, ask God to reveal His comfort to you. If you're in a season of relative ease, consider reaching out to someone who might need encouragement. Remember, our ultimate comfort comes not from the absence of suffering, but from God's presence in the midst of it.

Day 5: Eternal Comfort in God's Presence

Reading: Revelation 21:1-7

Devotional: As we conclude this devotional series, let's fix our eyes on the ultimate comfort that awaits us – eternal life in God's presence. This passage paints a beautiful picture of a restored world where there is no more death, sorrow, crying, or pain. While we enjoy many comforts in this life, they are but a shadow of the perfect comfort we'll experience in eternity with God. Today, allow this hope to put your current struggles and comforts in perspective. How might this eternal perspective change the way you approach your daily life? Pray for God to deepen your longing for His presence and to help you live in light of this future hope.

Small Group Guide

Opening Question: What's your favorite way to get comfortable? (e.g., favorite chair, food, activity)

Key Takeaways:

1. Comfort can become an idol when it absorbs our heart and imagination more than God.

2. God designed us for perfect comfort in Eden and promises its restoration in heaven.

3. Physical and emotional comfort are good gifts from God meant to be enjoyed with thanksgiving.

4. Comfort becomes an idol when we prioritize it over obedience to God.

Discussion Questions:

1. How do you see the pursuit of comfort influencing our society today?

2. Read Genesis 2:8-9 and Revelation 21:3-4. How does understanding God's original and future plan for our comfort impact your perspective on comfort in this life?

3. The sermon mentions that "We worship the gift instead of the Gift Giver." Can you think of examples where you've seen this happen in your own life or in others'?

4. Discuss the two litmus test questions for identifying comfort idolatry: a. Will I sin to get it? b. Will I sin if I don't get it? How can these questions help us examine our hearts?

5. Read the story of David and Bathsheba (2 Samuel 11:1-3). How did the pursuit of comfort lead David into sin? What lessons can we

learn from this?

6. How can we enjoy God's good gifts of comfort without turning them into idols?

7. In what areas of your life do you find it most challenging to balance enjoying comfort and maintaining spiritual discipline?

Additional Teaching

Finding Comfort in Suffering:

Suffering is an inevitable part of the human experience, yet it often perplexes us, leaving us questioning God's purpose in our pain. However, the Bible offers us profound insights into understanding suffering and finding comfort amid trials. In 2 Corinthians 1:3-7, the Apostle Paul gives us a rich framework for grasping how God uses our afflictions.

2 Corinthians 1:3-7 (NLT):
"3 All praise to God, the Father of our Lord Jesus Christ. God is our merciful Father and the source of all comfort. 4 He comforts us in all our troubles so that we can comfort others. When they are troubled, we will be able to give them the same comfort God has given us. 5 For the more we suffer for Christ, the more God will shower us with his comfort through Christ. 6 Even when we are weighed down with troubles, it is for your comfort and salvation! For when we ourselves are comforted, we will certainly comfort you. Then you can patiently endure the same things we suffer. 7 We are confident that as you share in our sufferings, you will also share in the comfort God gives us."

Questions for Reflection:

1. **What is the Source of True Comfort?**

Paul points us directly to God as the "source of all comfort." How does viewing God as the ultimate comforter change your perspective on the difficulties you face? Consider Isaiah 51:12, which says, "I, even I, am he who comforts you."

_____
_____
_____
_____

2. How Does Your Suffering Equip You to Help Others?

God's comfort is not just for our benefit; it enables us to "comfort others." When have you experienced God's comfort in such a way that it empowered you to help someone else? Reflect on Romans 12:15, which instructs us to "rejoice with those who rejoice; mourn with those who mourn."

3. What Role Does Community Play in Suffering?

Paul emphasizes mutual sharing in both suffering and comfort. How has your community of faith supported you in times of trouble? How can you be more intentional in providing comfort to others? Galatians 6:2 reminds us to "carry each other's burdens."

Modern Idols

4. Why Might God Allow Suffering in Your Life?

Verse 6 suggests that our trials can serve a greater purpose. How might God be using your current circumstances to shape your character or the lives of others? Reflect on James 1:2-4, which speaks of trials producing perseverance and maturity.

5. How Can You Foster a Spirit of Endurance?

Endurance is a recurring theme in Paul's letters. In your life, what practical steps can you take to grow in resilience and patience through suffering? Consider Hebrews 12:1, urging us to "run with perseverance the race marked out for us."

Additional Scriptures for Meditation:

- **Psalm 34:18 (NLT):**
  "The Lord is close to the brokenhearted; he rescues those whose spirits are crushed."

- **1 Peter 5:10 (NLT):**
  "In his kindness God called you to share in his eternal glory by means of Christ Jesus. So after you have suffered a little while, he will restore, support, and strengthen you, and he will place you on a firm foundation."

- **Romans 8:18 (NLT):**
  "Yet what we suffer now is nothing compared to the glory he will reveal to us later."

Practical Application:

- **Journaling**: Spend some time each day writing about your struggles and inviting God into those places of pain. Note instances where you experience His comfort.

- **Reach Out**: If you have been comforted by God in a particular area, seek out someone who is suffering similarly and offer them encouragement.

- **Prayer**: Ask God daily to use your experiences to not only grow your character but to be a light for others navigating their own valleys.

In every trial, remember that God's comfort is not just a distant promise but a present reality designed to overflow through us. May we open our hearts to His comfort and become conduits of His grace to others.

Meditative Prayer Reflection

Introduction: Before beginning this meditation, find a quiet and comfortable place where you can be undisturbed. Close your eyes, take a few deep breaths, and center your heart on experiencing God's presence and peace.

Opening Prayer: "Heavenly Father, You are the God of all comfort, the One who sees and knows every burden we carry. As we come to You in this moment, open our hearts to receive Your comforting presence. Help us to listen to Your voice and trust in Your promises. Amen."

Meditation:

1. **Recognition of God as Comforter:**
    - Inhale deeply and as you exhale, whisper, "God, my Comfort."
    - Reflect on God as your ultimate Comforter. Imagine His loving arms surrounding you, holding you close in your time of need.
    - Consider these words from 2 Corinthians 1:3, "All praise to God, the Father of our Lord Jesus Christ. God is our merciful Father and the source of all comfort."

2. **Receiving God's Comfort:**
    - As you breathe in, visualize breathing in God's peace. As you breathe out, let go of any tension or anxiety.
    - Quietly say, "Lord, I receive Your comfort." Allow His presence to fill the spaces of your heart that feel heavy or burdened.
    - Reflect on 1 Peter 5:7, "Cast all your anxiety on him

because he cares for you."

3. **Reflecting on Community:**
   - Picture the faces of those in your life who have supported you in difficult times. Offer a prayer of gratitude for their presence.
   - Consider how God might be calling you to comfort others with the comfort you have received. Ask for His guidance and strength.
   - Think about God's community and meditate on Galatians 6:2, "Carry each other's burdens, and in this way you will fulfill the law of Christ."

4. **Embracing Purpose in Suffering:**
   - Contemplate how your experiences of suffering might be woven into God's greater purpose for your life.
   - Ask God to reveal ways in which your trials can become testimonies of His grace and strength.
   - Reflect on Romans 8:28, "And we know that in all things God works for the good of those who love him, who have been called according to his purpose."

5. **Cultivating Endurance:**
   - Visualize yourself running a race, empowered by God's strength to endure all challenges.
   - Pray for perseverance and a hopeful heart, even when the road feels long and difficult.
   - Meditate on Hebrews 12:1, "Let us run with perseverance the race marked out for us."

Closing Prayer: Gracious Father, as we conclude this time of meditation, we thank You for Your enduring comfort and love. Inspire us to be vessels of Your peace to those around us. May our hearts remain open to Your guidance, and may we always seek You in every season of our lives. Thank You for being near, our ever-present help in times of trouble. Amen.

Reflection:

- When you are ready, take a moment to journal any thoughts or insights you received during this meditation. Consider how you might apply them to your life today.

_____
_____
_____
_____
_____
_____
_____
_____
_____
_____
_____
_____
_____
_____
_____
_____
_____
_____
_____
_____

Additional Teaching:

Light and Momentary Troubles

Life often brings challenges and difficulties that can feel overwhelming. Yet, the Apostle Paul provides us with a powerful example of maintaining perspective amidst trials. In his writings, Paul refers to these challenges as "light and momentary troubles" in the context of the eternal glory that awaits us. Let us explore how Paul was able to keep this perspective and how we can apply the same mindset in our lives.

Scriptural Foundation

2 Corinthians 4:16-18 (NIV):

"Therefore we do not lose heart. Though outwardly we are wasting away, yet inwardly we are being renewed day by day. For our light and momentary troubles are achieving for us an eternal glory that far outweighs them all. So we fix our eyes not on what is seen, but on what is unseen, since what is seen is temporary, but what is unseen is eternal."

Paul's Struggles

Paul's life was marked by numerous hardships, including imprisonment, beatings, shipwrecks, and constant danger (2 Corinthians 11:23-27). Despite these severe challenges, Paul maintained a perspective centered on God's eternal promises. His ability to see beyond the immediate pain to the glory of eternity provided him with strength and hope.

Why Paul Had a Different Perspective

Faith in Eternal Promises:

Paul was deeply rooted in the hope of eternal life with Christ. This hope allowed him to see his trials as temporary and insignificant in comparison to the eternal joy that awaited him.

Identity in Christ:

Paul's identity was firmly anchored in Christ rather than in his circumstances. This focus enabled him to view suffering as a part of the journey toward becoming more like Christ and experiencing His presence more fully.

Purpose through Suffering:

Paul understood that his trials served a greater purpose in God's plan. His sufferings allowed him to share in Christ's sufferings and helped spread the Gospel to others.

Application Questions

Reflect on Perspective:

What current challenges are you facing that seem overwhelming? How might viewing them in light of eternal glory change your perception?

_____
_____
_____
_____
_____
_____
_____
_____
_____
_____
_____

Anchoring in Hope:

How does the promise of eternal life with Christ influence your daily life and attitudes toward trials?

_____
_____

Identity Check:

In moments of difficulty, where do you find your identity? Is it in Christ, or have circumstances shaped it?

Purpose in Pain:

Consider a past challenge or suffering you endured. How did God use that experience for growth or to minister to others?

Conclusion

Paul's life teaches us that our troubles, while real, are temporary and leading us toward an incredible eternal reality. By fixing our eyes on the eternal unseen rather than the temporary seen, we gain strength and hope to endure life's challenges. Let Paul's perspective inspire us to live with an eternal mindset, finding purpose even in our trials and maintaining joy and hope through faith in God's promises.

Meditative Prayer Reflection

Begin by finding a quiet and comfortable place where you can sit or lie down without distractions. Close your eyes, take a deep breath, and allow your body to relax. Let this time be a sacred space between you and God, where you can reflect upon His word and presence.

Step 1: Invitation to God's Presence

Gently inhale, inviting the Holy Spirit to fill this moment. As you exhale, release any tension or worries.

Pray: "Lord, I invite Your presence here with me now. May Your peace fill this space as I seek to connect with You."

Step 2: Acknowledging the Reality of Troubles

Bring to mind any challenges or struggles you are currently facing. Hold them gently in your thoughts.

Pray: "Father, You see the troubles weighing on my heart. Acknowledge with me that these challenges are real, yet they are not beyond Your understanding or power."

Step 3: Focusing on the Eternal Perspective

Shift your thoughts to God's eternal promises. Picture the glory of eternity and the hope that surpasses all earthly trials.

Pray: "Help me, Lord, to fix my eyes not on what is seen, but on what is unseen. May Your promise of eternal life shine brightly in my mind, illuminating the path ahead with hope and peace."

Step 4: Reflecting on Paul's Example

Consider the Apostle Paul and his ability to endure suffering with an unwavering faith. Imagine his resilience and trust in God.

Pray: *"Father, let the example of Paul inspire me to hold fast to my faith. May I draw strength from his testimony, believing that You walk with me through every trial."*

Step 5: Affirming Identity and Purpose

Embrace your identity in Christ and the purpose God has placed on your life. Allow this truth to settle in your heart.

Pray: *"Anchor my identity in You, Jesus. Reveal to me the purpose in my pain, knowing that You are using every part of my story for Your glory and my good."*

Step 6: Offering Thanksgiving and Worship

With a heart of gratitude, lift up your thanks and worship to God for His continued presence and gifts.

Pray: *"As I breathe in, I receive Your love. As I breathe out, I offer my thanks. Every good and perfect gift comes from You, Father."*

Step 7: Closing Invitation

Open your hands as a symbol of surrender and readiness to receive God's strength and peace.

Pray: *"Lord, I surrender my troubles to You. Fill me with Your peace and equip me with the perspective I need to face today's challenges with faith and hope."*

Conclusion

Gently, bringing this prayer time to a close. Carry this sense of peace and perspective with you as you continue your day. May you always be mindful of the eternal glory that outshines all temporary troubles.

ABOUT THE AUTHOR

Kurt Barnes is the Lead Pastor of Silver Creek Fellowship Church in Silverton, Oregon. With a passion for guiding others in their spiritual journey, Kurt dedicates his life to serving his community and sharing the transformative power of God's love. He believes that God has a dream for each person's life, a plan filled with hope, purpose, and fulfillment. To learn more or listen to his messages, visit www.scf.tv.

Made in the USA
Columbia, SC
09 July 2025

60545152R00041